Shakespeare

A Collection of Quotations

Shakespeare
A Collection of Quotations

Edited by Jude Patterson

BARNES
& NOBLE
BOOKS

NEW YORK

The quotes in this book have been drawn from
THE OXFORD SHAKESPEARE and are assumed
to be accurate as quoted.

2004 Barnes & Noble Books

ISBN 0-7607-5360-1

Printed and bound in the United States of America

04 05 06 07 08 HC 9 8 7 6 5 4 3 2 1

To Kate

*Devise, wit; write, pen, for I am
for whole volumes, in folio.*
—ARMADO, *LOVE'S LABOUR'S LOST*, 1.2.175

Introduction

MAROONED ON A DESERT ISLAND WITH ONLY ONE BOOK
to read, more than a few castaways would choose
the complete works of Shakespeare. Charles Lamb
wrote in a letter to William Wordsworth: "Shakespeare
is one of the last books one should like to give up,
perhaps the one just before the Dying Service in a
large Prayer book." Virginia Woolf wrote in her diary:
"This is not 'writing' at all. Indeed, I could say that
Shakespeare surpasses literature altogether if I knew
what I meant." And Shakespearean actor Laurence
Olivier commented: "Shakespeare—the nearest thing
in incarnation to the eye of God." But it was the Bard's
fellow playwright Ben Jonson who had the foresight
to proclaim: "He was not of an age, but for all time!"
One can only imagine Jonson would be pleased that
Shakespeare's works have stood the test of time,
standing second only to the Bible in distribution
and quotation.

This collection of quotations brings together lines from Shakespeare's histories, comedies, and tragedies, and sprinkles them here and there with fragments from the poems and sonnets. The quotations are grouped into but seven simple topics—drama, human frailty, sorrow, magic, love, language, and death—and this collection is but a sliver from Shakespeare's canon (all quotations are from the 1987 edition of *The Complete Oxford Shakespeare*, edited by Stanley Wells and Gary Taylor, and changed only to Americanize British punctuation). Yet the full magnitude of Shakespeare's wit and soul shine through every line. We have to agree with Samuel Taylor Coleridge, who revising Jonson stated: "Shakespeare...is of no age—nor of any religion, or party or profession. The body and substance of his works came out of the unfathomable depths of his own oceanic mind." It is an ocean of infinite treasures.

Jude Patterson

All the world's a stage

MESSENGER.
For so your doctors hold it very meet,
Seeing too much sadness hath congealed your
    blood,
And melancholy is the nurse of frenzy.
Therefore they thought it good you hear a play
And frame your mind to mirth and merriment,
Which bars a thousand harms and lengthens
    life.
                    —*The Taming of the Shrew,* INDUCTION 2.127

1

CHORUS.
O for a muse of fire, that would ascend
The brightest heaven of invention:
A kingdom for a stage, princes to act,
And monarchs to behold the swelling scene.

—Henry V, PROLOGUE 1

THESEUS.
The poet's eye, in a fine frenzy rolling,
Doth glance from heaven to earth, from earth
    to heaven,
And as imagination bodies forth
The forms of things unknown, the poet's pen
Turns them to shapes, and gives to airy nothing
A local habitation and a name.

—A Midsummer Night's Dream, 5.1.12

CHORUS.
Can this cock-pit hold
The vasty fields of France? Or may we cram
Within this wooden O the very casques
That did affright the air at Agincourt?

—Henry V, PROLOGUE 11

CASSIUS.
How many ages hence
Shall this our lofty scene be acted over,
In states unborn and accents yet unknown!
BRUTUS.
How many times shall Caesar bleed in sport!

—Julius Caesar, 3.1.112

HAMLET.
Will you see the players well bestowed? Do ye
hear?—let them be well used, for they are the
abstracts and brief chronicles of the time.

—Hamlet, 2.2.524

POLONIUS.
The best actors in the world, either for tragedy,
comedy, history, pastoral, pastorical-comical,
historical-pastoral, tragical-historical, tragical-
comical-historical-pastoral, some individable
or poem unlimited. Seneca cannot be too heavy,
nor Plautus too light. For the law of writ and
the liberty, these are the only men.

—Hamlet, 2.2.397

QUINCE (as PROLOGUE).
If we offend, it is with our good will.
That you should think: we come not to offend
But with good will. To show our simple skill,
That is the true beginning of our end.

—A Midsummer Night's Dream, 5.1.108

CLEOPATRA.
When good will is showed, though't come
too short
The actor may plead pardon.

—Antony and Cleopatra, 2.5.8

CORIOLANUS.
Like a dull actor now
I have forgot my part, and I am out
Even to a full disgrace.

—Coriolanus, 5.3.40

HAMLET.

Speak the speech, I pray you, as I pronounced it to you—trippingly on the tongue; but if you mouth it, as many of your players do, I had as lief the town-crier had spoke my lines.

—*Hamlet*, 3.2.1

SIR TOBY.

Am not I consanguineous? Am I not of her blood? Tilly-vally—"lady"! "There dwelt a man in Babylon, lady, lady."

FESTE.

Beshrew me, the knight's in admirable fooling.

SIR ANDREW.

Ay, he does well enough if he be disposed, and so do I, too. He does it with a better grace, but I do it more natural.

—*Twelfth Night*, 2.3.74

VIOLA.

This fellow is wise enough to play the fool, And to do that well craves a kind of wit.

—*Twelfth Night*, 3.1.59

TOUCHSTONE.
I shall ne'er be ware of mine own wit till I break
my shins against it.

—*As You Like It,* 2.4.54

BOTTOM.
I grant you, friends, if you should fright the
ladies out of their wits they would have no
more discretion but to hang us, but I will
aggravate my voice so that I will roar you as
gently as any sucking dove. I will roar you an
'twere any nightingale.

—*A Midsummer Night's Dream,* 1.2.74

CLEOPATRA.
Antony
Shall be brought drunken forth, and I shall see
Some squeaking Cleopatra boy my greatness
I'th' posture of a whore.

—*Antony and Cleopatra,* 5.2.214

LORD.
And if the boy hath not a woman's gift
To rain a shower of commanded tears,
An onion will do well for such a shift,
Which, in a napkin being close conveyed,
Shall in despite enforce a watery eye.

—*The Taming of the Shrew,* INDUCTION 1.122

FALSTAFF.
Give me a cup of sack to make my eyes look
red, that it may be thought I have wept; for
I must speak in passion, and I will do it in
King Cambyses' vein.

—*1 Henry* IV, 2.5.387

BUCKINGHAM.
Tut, I can counterfeit the deep tragedian,
Tremble and start at wagging of a straw,
Speak, and look back, and pry on every side,
Intending deep suspicion; ghastly looks
Are at my service, like enforcèd smiles.

—*Richard III,* 3.5.5

ULYSSES.

Like a strutting player, whose conceit
Lies in his hamstring and doth think it rich
To hear the wooden dialogue and sound
'Twixt his stretched footing and the scaffoldage.

—Troilus and Cressida, 1.3.153

HAMLET.

Anything so overdone is from the purpose of
playing, whose end, both at the first and now,
was and is to hold as 'twere the mirror up to
nature, to show virtue her own feature, scorn
her own image, and the very age and body of
the time this form and pressure.

—Hamlet, 3.2.20

THESEUS.

The best in this kind are but shadows, and the
worst are no worse if imagination amend them.

—A Midsummer Night's Dream, 5.1.210

HAMLET.

I have heard that guilty creatures sitting at a play
Have by the very cunning of the scene
Been so struck to the soul that presently
They have proclaimed their malefactions.
. . . The play's the thing
Wherein I'll catch the conscience of the King.

—*Hamlet*, 2.2.590

THESEUS.

Is there no play
To ease the anguish of a torturing hour?

—*A Midsummer Night's Dream*, 5.1.36

LOUIS THE DAUPHIN.

There's nothing in this world can make me joy.
Life is as tedious as a twice-told tale,
Vexing the dull ear of a drowsy man.

—*King John*, 3.4.107

LEAR.

When we are born, we cry that we are come
To this great stage of fools.

—*King Lear*, 4.5.178

MACBETH.

Tomorrow, and tomorrow, and tomorrow
Creeps in this petty pace from day to day
To the last syllable of recorded time;
And all our yesterdays have lighted fools
The way to dusty death. Out, out, brief candle.
Life's but a walking shadow, a poor player
That struts and frets his hour upon the stage,
And then is heard no more. It is a tale
Told by an idiot, full of sound and fury;
Signifying nothing.

—Macbeth, 5.5.18

JAQUES.

All the world's a stage,
And all the men and women merely players.
They have their exits and their entrances,
And one man in his time plays many parts.

—As You Like It, 2.7.139

ANTONIO.

I hold the world but as the world, Graziano—

A stage where every man must play a part,

And mine a sad one.

—The Merchant of Venice, 1.1.77

LEAR.

Men must endure

Their going hence even as their coming hither.

Ripeness is all.

—King Lear, 5.2.9

JAQUES.

'Tis but an hour ago since it was nine,

And after one hour more 'twill be eleven.

And so from hour to hour we ripe and ripe,

And then from hour to hour we rot and rot;

And thereby hangs a tale.

—As You Like It, 2.7.24

HAMLET.

The play, I remember, pleased not the million.

'Twas caviare to the general.

—Hamlet, 2.2.437

EPILOGUE.

'Tis ten to one this play can never please
All that are here. Some come to take their ease,
And sleep an act or two.

—*Henry VIII*, Epilogue 1

FIRST SERVINGMAN.

My lord, you nod. You do not mind the play.

SLY.

Yes, by Saint Anne do I. A good matter, surely.
Comes there any more of it?

BARTHOLOMEW.

My lord, 'tis but begun.

—*The Taming of the Shrew*, 1.1.247

What a piece of work is a man!

BRUTUS.
There is a tide in the affairs of men
Which, taken at the flood, leads on to fortune;
Omitted, all the voyage of their life
Is bound in shallows and in miseries.

—*Julius Caesar*, 4.2.272

MENAS.

Who seeks and will not take when once 'tis
   offered

Shall never find it more.

—Antony and Cleopatra, 2.7.81

PROSPERO.

I find my zenith doth depend upon

A most auspicious star, whose influence

If now I court not, but omit, my fortunes

Will ever after droop.

—The Tempest, 1.2.182

CASSIUS.

Men at sometime were masters of their fates.

The fault, dear Brutus, is not in our stars,

But in ourselves, that we are underlings.

—Julius Caesar, 1.2.140

OTHELLO.

Who can control his fate?

—Othello, 5.2.272

PLAYER KING.
Our wills and fates do so contrary run
That our devices still are overthrown;
Our thoughts are ours, their ends none of
  our own.

—Hamlet, 3.2.202

HAMLET.
There's a divinity that shapes our ends,
Rough-hew them how we will.

—Hamlet, 5.2.10

GLOUCESTER.
As flies to wanton boys are we to th' gods;
They kill us for their sport.

—King Lear, 4.1.37

FLORIZEL.
So we profess
Ourselves to be the slaves of chance, and flies
Of every wind that blows.

—The Winter's Tale, 4.4.539

EDMOND.

This is the excellent foppery of the world: that
when we are sick in fortune—often the surfeits
of our own behaviour—we make guilty of our
disasters the sun, the moon, and stars; as if we
were villains on necessity, . . . and all that we are
evil in by a divine thrusting on. An admirable
evasion of whoremaster man, to lay his goatish
disposition on the charge of a star!

—*King Lear,* 1.2.116

HAMLET.

We defy augury. There's a special providence
in the fall of a sparrow. If it be now, 'tis not to
come. If it be not to come, it will be now. If it be
not now, yet it will come. The readiness is all.

—*Hamlet,* 5.2.165

EDMOND.
Men
Are as the time is.

—*King Lear,* 5.3.30

CLAUDIUS.
Take thy fair hour, Laertes. Time be thine,
And thy best graces spend it at thy will.

—Hamlet, 1.2.62

PISTOL.
Why, then, the world's mine oyster, which I with
sword will open.

—The Merry Wives of Windsor, 2.2.4

MOWBRAY.
The purest treasure mortal times afford
Is spotless reputation; that away,
Men are but gilded loam, or painted clay.
A jewel in a ten-times barred-up chest
Is a bold spirit in a loyal breast.
Mine honour is my life. Both grow in one.
Take honour from me, and my life is done.

—Richard II, 1.1.177

IAGO.
Good name in man and woman, dear my lord,
Is the immediate jewel of their souls.
Who steals my purse steals trash.

—*Othello*, 3.3.160

FIRST LORD DUMAINE.
The web of our life is of a mingled yarn, good
and ill together. Our virtues would be proud if
our faults whipped them not, and our crimes
would despair if they were not cherished by
our virtues.

—*All's Well That Ends Well*, 4.3.74

ANTONIO.
In nature there's no blemish but the mind.
None can be called deformed but the unkind.
Virtue is beauty.

—*Twelfth Night*, 3.4.359

ANTONY.

His life was gentle, and the elements
So mixed in him that nature might stand up
And say to all the world "This was a man."

—Julius Caesar, 5.5.72

MALVOLIO.

Be not afraid of greatness. Some are born great,
some achieve greatness, and some have greatness
thrust upon 'em.

—Twelfth Night, 2.5.139

HAMLET.

Assume a virtue if you have it not.

—Hamlet, 3.4.151

WOLSEY.

Be just, and fear not.
Let all the ends thou aim'st at be thy country's,
Thy God's, and truth's. Then if thou fall'st,

O Cromwell,
Thou fall'st a blessèd martyr.

—Henry VIII, 3.2.447

SECOND APPARITION.
Be bloody, bold, and resolute.

—Macbeth, 4.1.95

LUCIO.
I am a kind of burr; I shall stick.

—Measure for Measure, 4.3.172

NORFOLK.
Be to yourself
As you would to your friend.

—Henry VIII, 1.1.135

POLONIUS.
Neither a borrower nor a lender be,
For loan oft loses both itself and friend,
And borrowing dulls the edge of husbandry.
This above all—to thine own self be true,
And it must follow, as the night the day,
Thou canst not then be false to any man.

—Hamlet, 1.3.75

FOOL.

Have more than thou showest,

Speak less than thou knowest,

Lend less than thou owest,

Ride more than thou goest,

Learn more than thou trowest.

—King Lear, 1.4.117

PORTIA.

God made him, and therefore let him pass for
a man.

—The Merchant of Venice, 1.2.54

MACBETH.

I dare do all that may become a man;

Who dares do more is none.

—Macbeth, 1.7.46

CLAUDIO.

O, what men dare do! What men may do! What
men daily do, not knowing what they do!

—Much Ado About Nothing, 4.1.19

ISABELLA.

Man, proud man,

Dressed in a little brief authority,

Most ignorant of what he's most assured,

His glassy essence, like an angry ape

Plays such fantastic tricks before high heaven

As makes the angels weep.

—*Measure for Measure*, 2.2.120

HAMLET.

What a piece of work is a man! How noble in reason, how infinite in faculty, in form and moving how express and admirable, in action how like an angel, in apprehension how like a god—the beauty of the world, the paragon of animals!

—*Hamlet*, 2.2.304

WOLSEY.

This is the state of man. Today he puts forth
The tender leaves of hopes; tomorrow blossoms,
And bears his blushing honours thick upon him;
The third day comes a frost, a killing frost,
And when he thinks, good easy man, full surely
His greatness is a-ripening, nips his root,
And then he falls, as I do.

—*Henry VIII*, 3.2.353

O, woe is me!

When, in disgrace with Fortune and men's eyes,
I all alone beweep my outcast state,
And trouble deaf heaven with my bootless cries,
And look upon myself and curse my fate.

—Sonnet 29, 1

RICHARD.

O, that I were as great
As is my grief, or lesser than my name,
Or that I could forget what I have been,
Or not remember what I must be now!

—Richard II, 3.3.135

OPHELIA.

O, woe is me,
T'have seen what I have seen, see what I see!

—Hamlet, 3.1.163

NURSE.

O, she says nothing, sir, but weeps and weeps,
And now falls on her bed, and then starts up,
And "Tybalt" calls, and then on Romeo cries,
And then down falls again.

—Romeo and Juliet, 3.3.98

ANTONY.

Passion, I see, is catching, for mine eyes,
Seeing those beads of sorrow stand in thine,
Began to water.

—Julius Caesar, 3.1.286

LEAR.

You think I'll weep.

No, I'll not weep. I have full cause of weeping,
    Storm and tempest
But this heart shall break into a hundred
    thousand flaws
Or ere I'll weep.—O Fool, I shall go mad!

              —*King Lear,* 2.2.456

HAMLET.

O that this too too solid flesh would melt,
Thaw, and resolve itself into a dew.

              —*Hamlet,* 1.2.129

Though woe be heavy, yet it seldom sleeps,
And they that watch see time how slow it creeps.

         —*The Rape of Lucrece,* 1574

CLAUDIUS.

When sorrows come, they come not single spies,
But in battalions.

              —*Hamlet,* 4.5.76

GERTRUDE.

One woe doth tread upon another's heel,

So fast they follow.

—Hamlet, 4.7.135

FRIAR LAURENCE.

Affliction is enamoured of thy parts,

And thou art wedded to calamity.

—Romeo and Juliet, 3.3.2

JULIET.

Is there no pity sitting in the clouds

That sees into the bottom of my grief?

—Romeo and Juliet, 3.5.196

YORK.

Comfort's in heaven, and we are on the earth,

Where nothing lives but crosses, cares, and grief.

—Richard II, 2.2.78

MALCOLM.
Give sorrow words. The grief that does not
    speak
Whispers the o'erfraught heart and bids it break.

                         —*Macbeth,* 4.3.209

LEAR.
Howl, howl, howl, howl! O you are men
    of stones.
Had I your tongues and eyes, I'd use them so
That heaven's vault should crack.

                         —*King Lear,* 5.3.232

RICHARD.
My grief lies all within,
And these external manner of laments
Are merely shadows to the unseen grief
That swells with silence in the tortured soul.
There lies the substance.

                         —*Richard II,* 4.1.285

HAMLET.

To be, or not to be; that is the question:
Whether 'tis nobler in the mind to suffer
The slings and arrows of outrageous fortune,
Or to take arms against a sea of troubles,
And, by opposing, end them. To die, to sleep—
No more, and by a sleep to say we end
The heartache and the thousand natural shocks
That flesh is heir to—'tis a consummation
Devoutly to be wished. To die, to sleep.
To sleep, perchance to dream. Ay, there's the rub,
For in that sleep of death what dreams may come
When we have shuffled off this mortal coil
Must give us pause. There's the respect
That makes calamity of so long life,
For who would bear the whips and scorns
      of time,
Th'oppressor's wrong, the proud man's
      contumely,
The pangs of disprized love, the law's delay,
The insolence of office, and the spurns
That patient merit of th'unworthy takes,
When he himself might his quietus make

With a bare bodkin? Who would these fardels
    bear,
To grunt and sweat under a weary life,
But that the dread of something after death,
The undiscovered country from whose bourn
No traveller returns, puzzles the will,
And makes us rather bear those ills we have
Than fly to others that we know not of?
Thus conscience does make cowards of us all.

                                —*Hamlet,* 3.1.58

MACBETH.
Canst thou not minister to a mind diseased,
Pluck from the memory a rooted sorrow,
Raze out the written troubles of the brain,
And with some sweet oblivious antidote
Cleanse the fraught bosom of that perilous stuff
Which weighs upon the heart?
DOCTOR.
                            Therein the patient
Must minister to himself.
MACBETH.
Throw physic to the dogs; I'll none of it.

                              —*Macbeth,* 5.3.42

CLAUDIO.

The miserable have no other medicine
But only hope.

—*Measure for Measure*, 3.1.2

PAULINA.

What's gone and what's past help
Should be past grief.

—*The Winter's Tale*, 3.2.221

FALSTAFF.

A plague of sighing and grief—it blows a man up
like a bladder.

—*1 Henry IV*, 2.5.334

BUSHY.

Each substance of a grief hath twenty shadows
Which shows like grief itself but is not so.
For sorrow's eye, glazèd with blinding tears,
Divides one thing entire to many objects.

—*Richard II*, 2.2.14

LAFEU.

Moderate lamentation is the right of the dead,
excessive grief the enemy to the living.

COUNTESS.

If the living be not enemy to the grief, the excess
makes it soon mortal.

—*All's Well That Ends Well,* 1.1.52

BENEDICK.

Well, everyone can master a grief but he that
has it.

—*Much Ado About Nothing,* 3.2.26

MALCOLM.

Let us seek out some desolate shade, and there
Weep our sad bosoms empty.

—*Macbeth,* 4.3.1

ROMEO.

All these woes shall serve
For sweet discourses in our times to come.

—*Romeo and Juliet,* 3.5.52

COSTARD.

Affliction may one day smile again; and till then,
sit thee down, sorrow.

—*Love's Labours Lost*, 1.1.302

CLEON.

Shall we rest us here
And, by relating tales of others' griefs,
See if 'twill teach us to forget our own?

—*Pericles*, 4.1

RICHARD.

For God's sake, let us sit upon the ground,
And tell sad stories of the death of kings.

—*Richard II*, 3.2.151

TITUS.

Come and take choice of all my library,
And so beguile thy sorrow.

—*Titus Andronicus*, 4.1.34

JOHN OF GAUNT.

For gnarling sorrow hath less power to bite
The man that mocks at it and sets it light.

–*Richard II*, 1.3.281

Nature's infinite book of secrecy

LORENZO.
How sweet the moonlight sleeps upon this
    bank!
Here will we sit, and let the sounds of music
Creep in our ears. Soft stillness and the night
Become the touches of sweet harmony.

—*The Merchant of Venice, 5.1.54*

OBERON.
Thou rememb'rest
Since once I sat upon a promontory
And heard a mermaid on a dolphin's back
Uttering such dulcet and harmonious breath
That the rude sea grew civil at her song
And certain stars shot madly from their spheres
To hear the sea-maid's music.

—*A Midsummer Night's Dream*, 2.1.148

FERDINAND.
This music crept by me upon the waters,
Allaying both their fury and my passion
With its sweet air.

—*The Tempest*, 1.2.395

ARIEL.

Where the bee sucks, there suck I:

In a cowslip's bell I lie;

There I couch when owls do cry.

On the bat's back I do fly

After summer merrily.

Merrily, merrily shall I live now

Under the blossom that hangs on the bough.

—The Tempest, 5.1.88

AMIENS.

Under the greenwood tree

Who loves to lie with me,

And turn his merry note

Unto the sweet bird's throat,

Come hither, come hither, come hither.

Here shall he see

No enemy

But winter and rough weather.

—As You Like It, 2.5.1

KATHERINE'S GENTLEWOMAN.

Orpheus with his lute made trees,

And the mountain tops that freeze,

> Bow themselves when he did sing.

—Henry VIII, 3.1.3

TIMON.

Feast your ears with the music a while.

—Timon of Athens, 3.7.33

ARMADO.

Warble, child; make passionate my sense
of hearing.

—Love's Labour's Lost, 3.1.1

EVANS.

Jeshu pless me, how full of cholers I am, and trempling of mind! I shall be glad if he have deceived me. How melancholies I am! I will knog his urinals about his knave's costard when I have good opportunities for the 'ork. Pless my soul!—

> To shallow rivers, to whose falls
> Melodious birds sings madrigals.
> There will we make our peds of roses,
> And a thousand fragrant posies.

—*The Merry Wives of Windsor*, 3.1.11

THIRD FISHERMAN.

Master, I marvel how the fishes live in the sea.

MASTER.

Why, as men do a-land—the great ones eat up
    the little ones.

—*Pericles*, 5.67

CHARMIAN.

Is this the man? Is't you, sir, that know things?

SOOTHSAYER.

In nature's infinite book of secrecy

A little can I read.

—Antony and Cleopatra, 1.2.7

GLYNDWR.

I can call spirits from the vasty deep.

HOTSPUR.

Why, so can I, or so can any man;

But will they come when you do call for them?

—1 Henry IV, 3.1.51

ANTIGONUS.

I have heard, but not believed, the spirits
    o'th' dead

May walk again.

—The Winter's Tale, 3.3.15

SECOND WITCH.
By the pricking of my thumbs,
Something wicked this way comes.

—Macbeth, 4.1.61

PUCK.
Now it is the time of night
    That the graves, all gaping wide,
Every one lets forth his sprite
    In the churchway paths to glide.

—A Midsummer Night's Dream, 5.2.9

HAMLET.
'Tis now the very witching time of night,
When churchyards yawn, and hell itself breathes
    out
Contagion to this world.

—Hamlet, 3.2.377

BOLINGBROKE.

Deep night, dark night, the silent of the night,

The time of night when Troy was set on fire,

The time when screech-owls cry and bandogs
howl,

And spirits walk, and ghosts break up their
graves.

—*2 Henry VI,* 1.4.17

THREE WITCHES.

The weird sisters, hand in hand,

Posters of the sea and land,

Thus do go about, about,

Thrice to thine, and thrice to mine,

And thrice again, to make up nine.

Peace! The charm's wound up.

—*Macbeth,* 1.3.30

MARINER.

The skies look grimly

And threaten present blusters.

—*The Winter's Tale,* 3.3.3

TRINCULO.

I will here shroud till the dregs of the storm
be past.

—The Tempest, 2.2.39

LEAR.

Blow, winds, and crack your cheeks! Rage, blow,
You cataracts and hurricanoes, spout
Till you have drenched our steeples, drowned
    the cocks!

—King Lear, 3.2.1

CASCA.

Who ever knew the heavens menace so?

—Julius Caesar, 1.3.44

PERICLES.

Yet cease your ire, you angry stars of heaven!
Wind, rain, and thunder, remember earthly man
Is but a substance that must yield to you.

—Pericles, 5.41

CALIBAN.

Be not afeard. The isle is full of noises,

Sounds, and sweet airs, that give delight, and
hurt not.

Sometimes a thousand twangling instruments

Will hum about mine ears, and sometime voices

That if I then had waked after long sleep

Will make me sleep again; and then in dreaming

The clouds methought would open and show
riches

Ready to drop upon me, that when I waked

I cried to dream again.

—*The Tempest*, 3.2.138

HAMLET.

O God, I could be bounded in a nutshell and
count myself a king of infinite space, were it not
that I have bad dreams.

—*Hamlet,* 2.2.255

RICHARD.

Let not our babbling dreams affright our souls.

—*Richard III,* 5.6.38

THESEUS.

In the night imagining some fear,

How easy is a bush supposed a bear!

—A Midsummer Night's Dream, 5.1.21

FERDINAND.

'Tis fresh morning with me

When you are by at night.

—The Tempest, 3.1.33

HORATIO.

But look, the morn in russet mantle clad

Walks o'er the dew of yon high eastern hill.

—Hamlet, 1.1.147

DON PEDRO.

Look, the gentle day

Before the wheels of Phoebus round about

Dapples the drowsy east with spots of grey.

—Much Ado About Nothing, 5.3.25

MUSICIAN.

Hark, hark, the lark at heaven gate sings,
    And Phoebus gins arise,
His steeds to water at those springs
    On chaliced flowers that lies,
And winking Mary-buds begin to ope their
    golden eyes.

—Cymbeline, 2.3.19

PORTIA.

The crow doth sing as sweetly as the lark
When neither is attended, and I think
The nightingale, if she should sing by day,
When every goose is cackling, would be thought
No better a musician than the wren.
How many things by season seasoned are
To their right praise and true perfection!

—The Merchant of Venice, 5.1.102

FRIAR LAURENCE.

O mickle is the powerful grace that lies
In plants, herbs, stones, and their true qualities;
For naught so vile that on the earth doth live
But to the earth some special good doth give.

—Romeo and Juliet, 2.2.15

SALISBURY.

To gild refinèd gold, to paint the lily,
To throw a perfume on the violet,
To smooth the ice, or add another hue
Unto the rainbow, or with taper-light
To seek the beauteous eye of heaven to garnish,
Is wasteful and ridiculous excess.

—King John, 4.2.11

PROSPERO.
This rough magic
I here abjure. And when I have required
Some heavenly music—which even now I do—
To work mine end upon their senses that
This airy charm is for, I'll break my staff,
Bury it certain fathoms in the earth,
And deeper than did ever plummet sound
I'll drown my book.

—The Tempest, 5.1.50

What think you of falling in love?

ROSALIND.

There was never anything so sudden but the fight of two rams, and Caesar's thrasonical brag of "I came, saw, and overcame," for your brother and my sister no sooner met but they looked; no sooner looked but they loved; no sooner loved but they sighed; no sooner sighed but they asked one another the reason; no sooner knew the reason but they sought the remedy.

—*As You Like It,* 5.2.28

TRANIO.

Is it possible

That love should of a sudden take such hold?

—The Taming of the Shrew, 1.1.144

PHOEBE.

Who ever loved that loved not at first sight?

—As You Like It, 3.5.83

ONE FROM PORTIA'S TRAIN.

Tell me where is fancy bred,

Or in the heart, or in the head?

How begot, how nourishèd?

ALL.

Reply, reply.

—The Merchant of Venice, 3.2.63

THESEUS.

Lovers and madmen have such seething brains,

Such shaping fantasies, that apprehend

More than cool reason ever comprehends.

—A Midsummer Night's Dream, 5.1.4

VALENTINE.

How esteem'st thou me? I account of her beauty.

SPEED.

You never saw her since she was deformed.

VALENTINE.

How long hath she been deformed?

SPEED.

Ever since you loved her.

VALENTINE.

I have loved her ever since I saw her, and still
    I see her beautiful.

SPEED.

If you love her you cannot see her.

VALENTINE.

Why?

SPEED.

Because love is blind.

—The Two Gentlemen of Verona, 2.1.58

JESSICA.

Love is blind, and lovers cannot see
The pretty follies that themselves commit.

—The Merchant of Venice, 2.6.37

HELENA.

Love looks not with the eyes, but with the mind,
And therefore is winged Cupid painted blind.
Nor hath love's mind of any judgement taste;
Wings and no eyes figure unheedy haste.
And therefore is love said to be a child
Because in choice he is so oft beguiled.

—A Midsummer Night's Dream, 1.1.234

CRESSIDA.

To be wise and love
Exceeds man's might: that dwells with gods
    above.

—Troilus and Cressida, 3.2.152

VALENTINE.

Why, how know you that I am in love?

SPEED.

Marry, by these special marks: first, you have learned, like Sir Proteus, to wreath your arms, like a malcontent; to relish a love-song, like a robin redbreast; to walk alone, like one that had the pestilence; to sigh, like a schoolboy that had lost his ABC; to weep, like a young wench that had buried her grandam; to fast, like one that takes diet; to watch, like one that fears robbing; to speak puling, like a beggar at Hallowmas.

—*The Two Gentlemen of Verona*, 2.1.16

ROSALIND.

Your hose should be ungartered, your bonnet unbanded, your sleeve unbuttoned, your shoe untied, and everything about you demonstrating a careless desolation.

—*As You Like It*, 3.2.366

BIRON.

By heaven, I do love, and it hath taught me to rhyme and to be melancholy.

—*Love's Labour's Lost*, 4.3.11

ROMEO.

See how she leans her cheek upon her hand.
O, that I were a glove upon that hand,
That I might touch that cheek!

—*Romeo and Juliet*, 2.1.65

ULYSSES.

There's language in her eye, her cheek, her lip;
Nay, her foot speaks. Her wanton spirits look
    out
At every joint and motive of her body.

—*Troilus and Cressida*, 4.6.56

BEATRICE.

But for which of my good parts did you first
    suffer love for me?

BENEDICK.

Suffer love—a good epithet. I do suffer love
    indeed, for I love thee against my will.

              —*Much Ado About Nothing,* 5.2.58

ROSALIND.

What think you of falling in love?

CELIA.

Marry, I prithee do, to make sport withal; but
love no man in good earnest, nor no further in
sport neither than with safety of a pure blush
thou mayst in honour come off again.

              —*As You Like It,* 1.2.24

HELENA.

We cannot fight for love, as men may do;
We should be wooed, and were not made to woo.

       —*A Midsummer Night's Dream,* 2.1.241

EMILIA.

I know a lady in Venice would have walked
barefoot to Palestine for a touch of his nether lip.

—Othello, 4.3.36

LEONTES.

Is whispering nothing?
Is leaning cheek to cheek? Is meeting noses?
Kissing with inside lip? Stopping the career
Of laughter with a sigh?—a note infallible
Of breaking honesty. Horsing foot on foot?
Skulking in corners? Wishing clocks more swift,
Hours minutes, noon midnight? And all eyes
Blind with the pin and web but theirs, theirs
    only,
That would unseen be wicked? Is this nothing?
Why then the world and all that's in't is nothing!
The covering sky is nothing, Bohemia nothing,
My wife is nothing, nor nothing have these
    nothings
If this be nothing.

—The Winter's Tale, 1.2.287

BIRON.

Love's feeling is more soft and sensible

Than are the tender horns of cockled snails.

—Love's Labour's Lost, 4.3.313

ROMEO.

Is love a tender thing? It is too rough,

Too rude, too boist'rous, and it pricks like thorn.

—Romeo and Juliet, 1.4.25

LYSANDER.

For aught that I could ever read,

Could ever hear by tale or history,

The course of true love never did run smooth.

—A Midsummer Night's Dream, 1.1.132

JULIET.

Dost thou love me? I know thou wilt say "Ay,"

And I will take thy word. Yet if thou swear'st,

Thou mayst prove false. At lovers' perjuries,

They say, Jove laughs.

—Romeo and Juliet, 2.1.132

POLONIUS (reading letter from HAMLET to
     OPHELIA) .
"Doubt thou the stars are fire,
     Doubt that the sun doth move,
Doubt truth to be a liar,
     But never doubt I love."

—Hamlet, 2.2.116

KING HARRY.
Do you like me, Kate?
CATHERINE.
Pardonnez-mois, I cannot tell vat is "like me."
KING HARRY.
An angel is like you, Kate, and you are like
     an angel.

—Henry V, 5.2.106

BENEDICK.
When I said I would die a bachelor, I did not
think I should live till I were married.

—Much Ado About Nothing, 2.3.230

GREMIO.

He took the bride about the neck

And kissed her lips with such a clamorous
    smack

That at the parting all the church did echo.

—The Taming of the Shrew, 3.3.50

JOHN.

He is the half part of a blessèd man,

Left to be finishèd by such as she;

And she a fair divided excellence,

Whose fullness of perfection lies in him.

—King John, 2.1.438

PORTIA.

One half of me is yours, the other half yours—

Mine own, I would say; but if mine, then yours,

And so all yours.

—The Merchant of Venice, 3.2.16

PORTIA.

Am I your self

But as it were in sort or limitation?

To keep with you at meals, comfort your bed,

And talk to you sometimes? Dwell I but in the
    suburbs

Of your good pleasure? If it be no more,

Portia is Brutus' harlot, not his wife.

BRUTUS.

You are my true and honourable wife,

As dear to me as are the ruddy drops

That visit my sad heart.

—Julius Caesar, 2.1.281

To me, fair friend, you never can be old;

For as you were when first your eye I eyed,

Such seems your beauty still.

—Sonnet 104, 1

JULIET.

My bounty is as boundless as the sea,

My love as deep. The more I give to thee

The more I have, for both are infinite.

—Romeo and Juliet, 2.1.175

And ruined love when it is built anew
Grows fairer than at first, more strong,
    far greater.

—*Sonnet 119, 11*

Let me not to the marriage of true minds
Admit impediments. Love is not love
Which alters when it alteration finds,
Or bends with the remover to remove.
O, no, it is an ever-fixèd mark
That looks on tempests and is never shaken;
It is the star to every wand'ring barque,
Whose worth's unknown, although his height
    be taken.
Love's not time's fool, though rosy lips and
    cheeks
Within his bending sickle's compass come;
Love alters not with his brief hours and weeks,
But bears it out even to the edge of doom.
    If this be error and upon me proved,
    I never writ, nor no man ever loved.

—*Sonnet 116*

The King's English

HARRY.
These fellows of infinite tongue, that can rhyme themselves into ladies' favours, they do always reason themselves out again.

—Henry V, 5.2.156

TROILUS.
Words, words, mere words, no matter from the
    heart.

—Troilus and Cressida, 5.3.111

BENEDICK.

I do much wonder that one man, seeing how much another man is a fool when he dedicates his behaviours to love, will, after he hath laughed at such shallow follies in others, become the argument of his own scorn by falling in love. And such a man is Claudio…
He was wont to speak plain and to the purpose, like an honest man and a soldier; and now is he turned orthography. His words are a very fantastical banquet, just so many strange dishes.

—*Much Ado About Nothing,* 2.3.8

MISTRESS QUICKLY.

Here will be an old abusing of God's patience and the King's English.

—*The Merry Wives of Windsor,* 1.4.4

EVANS.

I pray you have your remembrance, child.
Accusativo: "hing, hang, hog."
MISTRESS QUICKLY.

"Hang-hog" is Latin for bacon, I warrant you.

—*The Merry Wives of Windsor,* 4.1.41

ARMADO.

Remuneration—O, that's the Latin word for
three-farthings.

—*Love's Labour's Lost,* 3.1.133

FIRST PLAYER.

"But who, O who had seen the mobbled
    queen"—
HAMLET.

"The mobbled queen"?
POLONIUS.

That's good; "mobbled queen" is good.

—*Hamlet,* 2.2.504

COSTARD. O, they have lived long on the alms-basket of words. I marvel thy master hath not eaten thee for a word; for thou art not so long by the head as *honorificabilitudinitatibus*. Thou art easier swallowed than a flapdragon.

—Love's Labour's Lost, 5.1.38

CELIA.
Well said. That was laid on with a trowel.

—As You Like It, 1.2.99

HORATIO.
These are but wild and whirling words.

—Hamlet, 1.5.137

HAMLET.
A rhapsody of words.

—Hamlet, 3.4.47

BASTARD.
Zounds! I was never so bethumped with words
Since I first called my brother's father Dad.

—King John, 2.1.467

KATHERINE.

Where did you study all this goodly speech?

PETRUCCIO.

It is extempore, from my mother-wit.

—*The Taming of the Shrew,* 2.1.257

LORD SANDS.

If I chance to talk a little wild, forgive me;

I had it from my father.

—*Henry VIII,* 1.4.26

FERDINAND.

A man...

That hath a mint of phrases in his brain.

—*Love's Labour's Lost,* 1.1.162

BIRON.

Taffeta phrases, silken terms precise,

    Three-piled hyperboles, spruce affectation,

Figures pedantical—these summer flies

    Have blown me full of maggot ostentation..

—*Love's Labour's Lost,* 5.2.407

CLAUDIUS.

My words fly up, my thoughts remain below.

Words without thoughts never to heaven go.

—Hamlet, 3.3.97

HENRY.

'Tis well said again,

And 'tis a kind of good deed to say well—

And yet words are no deeds.

—Henry VIII, 3.2.153

FESTE.

A sentence is but a cheverel glove to a good

wit, how quickly the wrong side may be turned

outward.

VIOLA.

Nay, that's certain. They that dally nicely with

words may quickly make them wanton.

—Twelfth Night, 3.1.11

FALSTAFF.

Have I lived to stand at the taunt of one that

makes fritters of English?

—The Merry Wives of Windsor, 5.5.141

FESTE.

Leave thy vain bibble-babble.

—Twelfth Night, 4.2.98

ANTONIO.

The devil can cite Scripture for his purpose.

An evil soul producing holy witness

Is like a villain with a smiling cheek,

A goodly apple rotten at the heart.

O, what a goodly outside falsehood hath!

—The Merchant of Venice, 1.3.97

OCTAVIUS.

I do not much dislike the matter, but

The manner of his speech.

—Antony and Cleopatra, 2.2.116

TITUS.

These words are razors to my wounded heart.

—Titus Andronicus, 1.1.311

BENEDICK.

She speaks poniards, and every word stabs.

—Much Ado About Nothing, 2.1.231

LEAR.

Mend your speech a little

Lest you may mar your fortunes.

—King Lear, 1.1.93

CLEOPATRA.

Though it be honest, it is never good

To bring bad news. Give to a gracious message

An host of tongues, but let ill tidings tell

Themselves when they be felt.

—Antony and Cleopatra, 2.5.85

DON PEDRO.

He hath a heart as sound as a bell, and his

tongue is the clapper, for what his heart thinks

his tongue speaks.

—Much Ado About Nothing, 3.2.11

LEAR.

Her voice was ever soft,

Gentle, and low, an excellent thing in woman.

—King Lear, 5.3.247

CANTERBURY.

When he speaks,

The air, a chartered libertine, is still,

And the mute wonder lurketh in men's ears

To steal his sweet and honeyed sentences.

—Henry V, 1.1.48

NORTHUMBERLAND.

Your fair discourse hath been as sugar,

Making the hard way sweet and delectable.

—Richard II, 2.3.6

OTHELLO.

Rude am I in my speech,

And little blessed with the soft phrase of peace.

—Othello, 1.3.81

CASSIUS.

This rudeness is a sauce to his good wit,

Which gives men stomach to digest his words

With better appetite.

—Julius Caesar, 1.2.300

ANTONY.

For I have neither wit, nor words, nor worth,

Action, nor utterance, nor the power of speech,

To stir men's blood. I only speak right on.

—Julius Caesar, 3.2.216

MIRANDA.

Your tale, sir, would cure deafness.

—The Tempest, 1.2.107

ELIZABETH.

An honest tale speeds best being plainly told.

—Richard III, 4.4.289

POLONIUS.

Brevity is the soul of wit.

—Hamlet, 2.2.91

VIOLA.

I would be loath to cast away my speech, for
besides that it is excellently well penned, I have
taken great pains to con it.

—Twelfth Night, 1.5.165

Farewell!

HECTOR.
The end crowns all,
And that old common arbitrator Time
Will one day end it.

—Troilus and Cressida, 4.7.107

SALISBURY.
O, call back yesterday, bid time return.

—Richard II, 3.2.65

PROSPERO.

Our revels now are ended. These our actors,
As I foretold you, were all spirits, and
Are melted into air, into thin air;
And like the baseless fabric of this vision,
The cloud-capped towers, the gorgeous palaces,
The solemn temples, the great globe itself,
Yea, all which it inherit, shall dissolve;
And, like this insubstantial pageant faded,
Leave not a rack behind. We are such stuff
As dreams are made on, and our little life
Is rounded with a sleep.

—*The Tempest,* 4.1.148

ULYSSES.

Time hath, my lord,
A wallet at his back, wherein he puts
Alms for oblivion...
For beauty, wit,
High birth, vigour of bone, desert in service,
Love, friendship, charity, are subjects all
To envious and calumniating time.
One touch of nature makes the whole world kin.

—*Troilus and Cressida,* 3.3.139

FESTE.

Why, "Some are born great, some achieve greatness, and some have greatness thrown upon them."...and thus the whirligig of time brings in his revenges.

—*Twelfth Night,* 5.1.367

WOLSEY.

I have touched the highest point of all my
    greatness,
And from that full meridian of my glory
I haste now to my setting. I shall fall
Like a bright exhalation in the evening,
And no man see me more.

—*Henry VIII,* 3.2.224

ROMEO.

My mind misgives
Some consequence yet hanging in the stars
Shall bitterly begin his fearful date
With this night's revels, and expire the term
Of a despisèd life, closed in my breast,
By some vile forfeit of untimely death.

—*Romeo and Juliet,* 1.4.106

MACDUFF.

Shake off this downy sleep, death's counterfeit,
And look on death itself.

—Macbeth, 2.3.76

RICHARD.

For within the hollow crown
That rounds the mortal temples of a king
Keeps Death his court; and there the antic sits,
Scoffing his state and grinning at his pomp,
Allowing him a breath, a little scene
To monarchize, be feared, and kill with looks,
Infusing him with self and vain conceit,
As if this flesh which walls about our life
Were brass impregnable; and humoured thus,
Comes at the last, and with a little pin
Bores through his castle wall; and farewell, king.

—Richard II, 3.2.157

CLAUDIO.

Ay, but to die, and go we know not where;

To lie in cold obstruction, and to rot;

This sensible warm motion to become

A kneaded clod, and the dilated spirit

To bathe in fiery floods…'tis too horrible!

—*Measure for Measure,* 3.1.118

CAESAR.

Of all the wonders that I yet have heard,

It seems to me most strange that men should
    fear,

Seeing that death, a necessary end,

Will come when it will come.

—*Julius Caesar,* 2.2.34

JOHN OF GAUNT.

More are men's ends marked than their lives
    before.

The setting sun, and music at the close,

As the last taste of sweets, is sweetest last,

Writ in remembrance more than things long
    past.

—*Richard II,* 2.1.11

ANTONY.

Friends, Romans, countrymen, lend me your
    ears.
I come to bury Caesar, not to praise him.
The evil that men do lives after them;
The good is oft interrèd with their bones.
So let it be with Caesar.

—Julius Caesar, 3.2.74

OTHELLO.

I pray you, in your letters,
When you shall these unlucky deeds relate,
Speak of me as I am. Nothing extenuate,
Nor set down aught in malice. Then must you
    speak
Of one that loved not wisely but too well.

—Othello, 5.2.349

BENEDICK.

If a man do not erect in this age his own tomb
ere he dies, he shall live no longer in monument
than the bell rings and the widow weeps.

—Much Ado About Nothing, 5.2.69

RICHARD.

Let's talk of graves, of worms and epitaphs,
Make dust our paper, and with rainy eyes
Write sorrow on the bosom of the earth.
Let's choose executors and talk of wills.

—Richard II, 3.2.141

Item, I give unto my wife my second best bed,
with the furniture.

—Shakespeare's will, 1616

CLEOPATRA.

Give me my robe. Put on my crown. I have
Immortal longings in me.

—Antony and Cleopatra, 5.2.275

GLOUCESTER.

O, let me kiss that hand!

LEAR.

Let me wipe it first; it smells of mortality.

GLOUCESTER.

O ruined piece of nature! This great world
Shall so wear out to naught.

—King Lear, 4.5.128

CLIFFORD.

Here burns my candle out—ay, here it dies,

Which, whiles it lasted, gave King Henry light.

—*3 Henry VI*, 2.6.1

ANTONY.

I am dying, Egypt, dying. Only

I here importune death awhile until

Of many thousand kisses the poor last

I lay upon thy lips.

—*Antony and Cleopatra*, 4.16.18

CHARMIAN.

So, fare the well.

Now boast thee, death, in thy possession lies

A lass unparalleled. Downy windows, close,

And golden Phoebus never be beheld

Of eyes again so royal.

—*Antony and Cleopatra*, 5.2.308

CAPULET.

Death lies on her like an untimely frost

Upon the sweetest flower of all the field.

—*Romeo and Juliet*, 4.4.55

LAERTES.

Lay her i'th' earth,

And from her fair and unpolluted flesh

May violets spring.

—Hamlet, 5.1.233

ROMEO.

O, here

Will I set up my everlasting rest

And shake the yoke of inauspicious stars

From this world-wearied flesh. Eyes, look your
    last.

Arms, take your last embrace, and lips, O you

The doors of breath, seal with a righteous kiss

A dateless bargain to engrossing death.

—Romeo and Juliet, 5.3.109

HORATIO.

Now cracks a noble heart. Good night, sweet
    prince,

And flights of angels sing thee to thy rest.

—Hamlet, 5.2.312

KENT.

Vex not his ghost. O, let him pass. He hates him
That would upon the rack of this tough world
Stretch him out longer.

—King Lear, 5.3.289

No longer mourn for me when I am dead
Than you shall hear the surly sullen bell
Give warning to the world that I am fled
From this vile world with vilest worms to dwell.

—Sonnet 71, 1

OPHELIA.

I hope all will be well. We must be patient. But I
cannot choose but weep to think they should
lay him i'th' cold ground. My brother shall know
of it. And so I thank you for your good counsel.
Come, my coach! Good night, ladies, good
night, sweet ladies, good night, good night.

—Hamlet, 4.5.67

OLD MAN.

God's benison go with you, and with those

That would make good of bad, and friends of
    foes.

—Macbeth, 2.4.41

ANTONIO.

The gentleness of all the gods go with thee!

—Twelfth Night, 2.1.39

MARGARET.

O, go not yet. Even thus two friends condemned

Embrace, and kiss, and take ten thousand
    leaves,

Loather a hundred times to part than die.

Yet now farewell, and farewell life with thee.

—2 Henry VI, 3.3.357

QUEEN.

And must we be divided? Must we part?

RICHARD.

Ay, hand from hand, my love, and heart from
    heart.

—Richard II, 5.1.81

DUCHESS OF GLOUCESTER.

Art thou gone too? All comfort go with thee,
For none abides with me.

—2 Henry VI, 2.4.88

BOLINGBROKE.

This must my comfort be:
That sun that warms you here shall shine on me.

—Richard II, 1.3.138

ANTONY.

Come. Our separation so abides and flies
That thou residing here goes yet with me,
And I hence fleeting, here remain with thee.

—Antony and Cleopatra, 1.3.103

GHOST.

Adieu, adieu, Hamlet. Remember me.

HAMLET.

...Remember thee?
Ay, thou poor ghost, while memory holds a seat
In this distracted globe.

—Hamlet, 1.5.91

86